Pegasus the Winged Horse

Written by C.J. Naden
Illustrated by Robert Baxter

Troll Associates

Pronunciation Guide

Athena	(uh-THEE-nuh)
Bellerophon	(buh-LER-uh-fon)
Chimaera	(ky-MEER-uh)
Iobates	(eye-OBE-uh-teez)
Olympus	(oh-LIM-pus)
Pegasus	(PEG-uh-sus)
Poseidon	(poe-SY-dun)
Proetus	(pro-EE-tus)
Zeus	(ZOOSS)

Long ago in Ancient Greece, there was a very special horse called Pegasus. He was special because he could fly. Pegasus had great snowy wings that lifted him right into the clouds. Sometimes he played games in the clouds, gliding from one to the other like a big white bird.

3

Everyone on earth loved Pegasus because he was such a beautiful and gentle horse. And he was a favorite, too, with the gods and goddesses who lived high on Mount Olympus.

When he was not in the clouds, Pegasus loved to eat sweet green grasses on earth. And sometimes people would see him drinking cool water from a bubbling spring. But they could never get too close. If they did, Pegasus would perk up his snowy head and look around. And if they stepped closer, he would lift his wings and fly away.

A young man called Bellerophon loved to watch Pegasus. Bellerophon was the son of a King. But people whispered that his true father was Poseidon, the powerful god of the sea. Bellerophon heard the whispers, and he began to wonder if they were true. "If my real father is a god, then *I* am a god," Bellerophon thought.

Bellerophon began to think of himself as a god. And he wanted to be as famous as all the other gods. How could he do that? Then an idea came to him. Pegasus! Bellerophon certainly would be famous if he could capture the winged horse. But how? Who could capture a flying horse?

Bellerophon decided to sleep one night in the temple of Athena. She was the goddess of wisdom and warfare. Perhaps the powerful goddess had heard of his wish to tame the flying horse. Perhaps she would help him.

When Bellerophon awoke the next morning, he looked around. Was there a sign from Athena? Then he saw it. On the ground, gleaming in the first rays of the morning sun, lay a golden bridle. Bellerophon shouted for joy. "Athena has heard me!" he cried. "Now I will capture Pegasus."

Bellerophon spent the next few days searching for the beautiful horse. Then, early one morning, he saw Pegasus drinking water from a spring. Slowly, Bellerophon moved forward. In his hand, he held the golden bridle.

Bellerophon went closer and closer to Pegasus. Suddenly, the horse raised his snowy head. Bellerophon could scarcely breathe. Would Pegasus fly away? But no! He only shook his mane and nodded in friendship. Then he went on drinking from the spring. Athena's magic had worked.

Quietly, Bellerophon slipped the golden bridle over the head of Pegasus. The winged horse shook his mane again. But he did not run. Finally, Bellerophon climbed upon his back. And off they flew into the blue morning sky, soaring above the tree tops. Bellerophon felt that he could touch the clouds!

12

With his wonderful winged horse, Bellerophon now thought
of himself as master of the land and sky. But he still felt that
his name was not as famous as the gods. What brave deed
could he do? What would bring his name to all people every-
where?

Bellerophon and Pegasus went off in search of fame and adventure. One day they visited the land of King Proetus. The King had heard of Bellerophon and his marvelous horse. He gladly welcomed his visitors. Before long, the handsome Bellerophon became a great favorite at the court. But the King was a jealous man. He decided to get rid of this unwanted stranger.

14

A guest in Ancient Greece was a special person. Harm your guest and the gods would surely punish you. So Proetus could not kill Bellerophon himself. "But King Iobates owes me a favor," thought Proetus. "I will let *him* kill Bellerophon!"

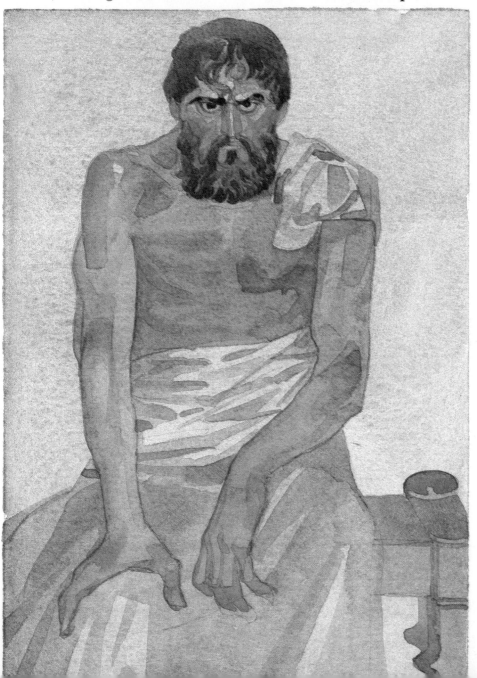

Proetus asked Bellerophon to take a letter to King Iobates. But King Iobates was very unhappy when he read it. It was true that he did owe Proetus a favor. But now Bellerophon was a guest in *his* house. Iobates was not going to kill the man and earn the punishment of the gods. What could he do?

Then Iobates had an idea. He would send Bellerophon on so dangerous a journey that he would never return. "You wish to be as famous as the gods," said the King to Bellerophon. "Then kill the dreaded Chimaera. If you do this, you will be the most famous man in the country."

The Chimaera was the most dreadful of all monsters. This huge beast was part lion, part goat, and part dragon. It breathed flames, and it tore apart its victims with great grasping claws. Iobates knew that Bellerophon could never destroy the Chimaera.

Bellerophon and Pegasus flew to the top of a high mountain where the Chimaera lived. Long streaks of flame shot from its nostrils. Sharp fangs reached high into the air. The Chimaera was a frightening sight. But King Iobates had forgotten about Pegasus!

19

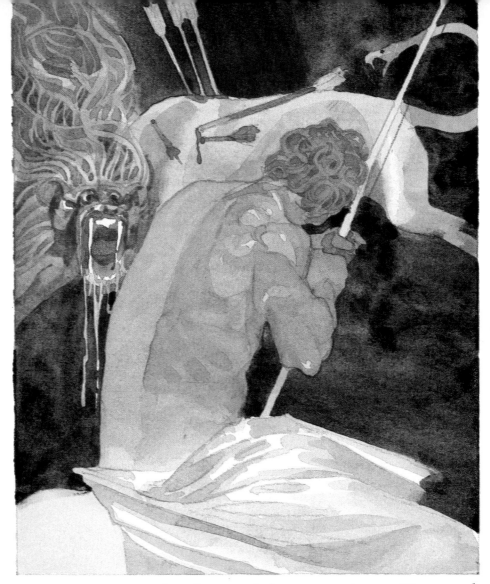

Pegasus flew around and around the mountaintop. He stayed always just out of reach of the grasping claws and streaks of flame. When the beast grew dizzy from trying to grab the winged horse, Bellerophon shot his arrows into the body of the Chimaera. It was over in minutes. The Chimaera was dead!

King Iobates could not believe his eyes when Bellerophon returned. He was so impressed that he praised Bellerophon and
invited him to stay in his kingdom. Bellerophon did so, and he
performed other deeds for the King. Soon everyone was prais-
ing the great warrior and talking about his bravery.

Bellerophon was now the greatest hero in the land. People crowded about his chariot in the streets. They pushed each other aside just to touch the hem of his clothing. In time, he married the beautiful daughter of King Iobates. He had wealth and luxury. And, of course, he had the wonder horse, Pegasus.

22

But all this did not satisfy Bellerophon. People thought he was a great hero, yes. But they still did not think he was a god. Gods did not walk the earth. They lived on the high peaks of Mount Olympus. "Very well," thought Bellerophon, "I shall live on Olympus, too."

Snow-capped Mount Olympus was a glorious land where rain never fell and winds never blew. The immortal gods and goddesses remained ever young and beautiful. They spent their days in happiness among the fragrant gardens.

Bellerophon knew that only rarely did the gods invite a mortal to Olympus. "But I am a god, too," he thought, "and I am a great hero. Surely the gods will be happy to have me join them on Mount Olympus."

Once Bellerophon had decided to go to Mount Olympus, he knew that Pegasus must take him there. So, each day when Bellerophon and Pegasus flew out in the blue sky, Bellerophon urged the winged horse higher and higher. Each day they flew closer and closer to the forbidden home of the gods.

Pegasus knew that something was wrong. It was not possible for a mortal to invade the home of the gods. So each time that Bellerophon urged him on, Pegasus would shake his great snowy mane and swoop down to earth. Time and time again, Bellerophon urged Pegasus up to Olympus. But Pegasus would not go.

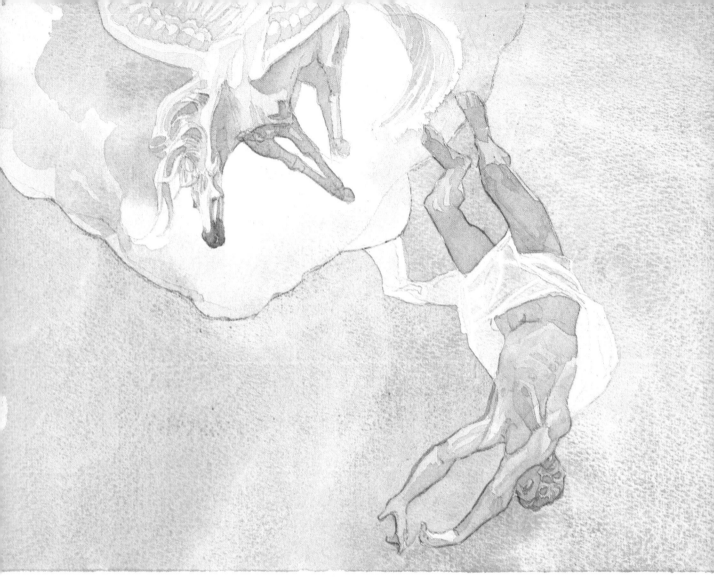

Then one day, Bellerophon rode the horse higher than ever before. When Pegasus realized it, they were nearly at the gates of Mount Olympus. "Take me inside! Take me inside!" cried Bellerophon. But Pegasus could not. Instead, he did the only thing he knew. He reared up, sending his rider crashing to earth far below.

Bellerophon lived, but he was no longer a hero. He was no longer a warrior. His body was broken and so was his spirit. Never again would he dash into battle. Never again would he ride the great horse across the cloud-filled sky. Bellerophon had earned the hatred of the gods. And they had punished him.

Bellerophon had been a great hero. He had fame and riches and the wonderful Pegasus. Now he had nothing. He wandered alone and unhappy. Finally, he died. But no one knows where or when.

The gods punished Bellerophon, but they rewarded the gentle
Pegasus. They brought him to Mount Olympus. He was given
an honored place in the golden stable of Zeus. Sometimes
when mighty Zeus became angry, he would call for Pegasus.
The great horse would bring bolts of lightning to the god.
Then Zeus would hurl the lightning to the earth.

From time to time, Pegasus returned to earth himself. He still loved the taste of fresh, green grass and sweet spring water. Then he would lift his snowy head and soar once more into the sky. Pegasus had won what Bellerophon would never have — a place among the gods.